KUNDALINI
THE SECRET OF LIFE

SWAMI
MUKTANANDA

KUNDALINI
THE SECRET OF LIFE

A SIDDHA YOGA PUBLICATION
PUBLISHED BY THE SYDA FOUNDATION

Published by SYDA Foundation
371 Brickman Road, PO Box 600, South Fallsburg, NY 12779-0600

Second Edition, 1994

Cover Illustration by Shane Conroy

Printed in the United States of America

ISBN: 0-911307-34-6

CONTENTS

Swami Muktananda

SWAMI MUKTANANDA
and the Lineage of Siddha Yoga Masters

Swami Muktananda was born in 1908 to a prosperous family
of landowners near the South Indian city of Mangalore. At
around the age of fifteen, he had several encounters with the
great saint, Bhagawan Nityananda, whom he would later recognize as his spiritual Master. These encounters were a turn-
ing point for the boy. Shortly thereafter, he decided to set out
from home in search of direct experience of God, a journey
that would ultimately take him three times across the length
and breadth of India and last almost a quarter of a century.
He met his first teacher, Siddharudha Swami, who was one of
the renowned scholars and saints of that time, in an ashram
in Hubli, two hundred miles to the north of his parents'
home. It was there that he studied Vedanta, took the vows of
sannyāsa, or monkhood, and received the name Swami
Muktananda, "the bliss of liberation."

When Siddharudha died, in 1929, Swami Muktananda
began to visit one ashram after another, meeting and learning
from more than sixty spiritual teachers, always looking for the
one who would give him the experience of God. He searched
for eighteen years. In that time he mastered the major scriptures of India, received training in an array of disciplines and
skills — from hatha yoga to cooking and *ayurvedic* medicine
— and still he did not find what he sought.

At last one of the saints he met sent him to Bhagawan
Nityananda, the Siddha Master, or perfected spiritual teacher,

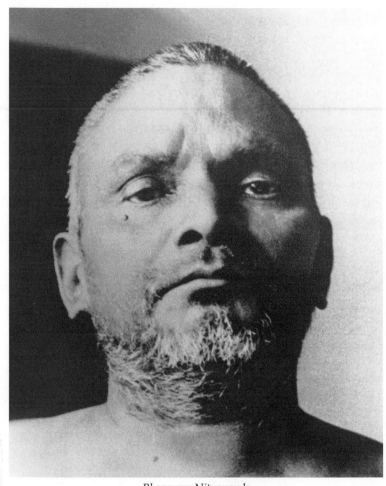

Bhagawan Nityananda

he had encountered so many years before. Bhagawan Nityananda was then living in the tiny village of Ganeshpuri, fifty miles northeast of Bombay. Recognizing Bhagawan Nityananda as the Guru he had been seeking, Swami Muktananda later said that this meeting "ended my wandering forever." From Bhagawan Nityananda he received Shaktipat, the sacred initiation of the Siddhas by which one's inner spiritual energy is awakened. This energy, known as Kundalini, is a divine potential that exists within each human being; once awakened, it enables a seeker to reach the most subtle levels of inner experience.

With his initiation, Swami Muktananda became a disciple, dedicating himself to the spiritual path set forth by his Guru. This was the beginning of nine years of intense transformation, during which Muktananda underwent total purification, explored the inner realms of consciousness, and finally became steady in his experience of the fullness and ecstasy of his own innermost nature. In 1956 Bhagawan Nityananda declared that his disciple's inner journey was complete: Swami Muktananda had attained Self-realization, the experience of union with God.

Even after he had attained the goal of his discipleship, Swami Muktananda remained a devoted disciple, continuing to live quietly near Ganeshpuri. Bhagawan Nityananda established him in a small ashram near his own, and for five years, Guru and disciple lived less than a mile from each other. Then in 1961, just before his death, Bhagawan Nityananda passed on to Swami Muktananda the grace-bestowing power of the Siddha Masters, investing him with the capacity to give spiritual awakening to others. On that day, Bhagawan Nityananda told him, "The entire world will see you."

In the decades that followed, Baba, as Swami Muktananda came to be known, traveled throughout the world, imparting to others the same Shaktipat initiation he himself had received and introducing seekers to the spontaneous yoga of the Siddha

Swami Chidvilasananda

Masters. He freely bestowed the grace his Guru had given to him, opening to unprecedented numbers of people what he called "the royal road" of Siddha Yoga — a wide and accessible path to God. People who had never before heard of meditation found that in Baba's presence they were drawn into an inner stillness that gave their lives new focus and meaning. He introduced programs to give Shaktipat initiation to vast groups and tirelessly explained to people the ongoing process of transformation that was unfolding within them. As Baba became world renowned, his ashram (now known as Gurudev Siddha Peeth) expanded to accommodate the visiting seekers, and in time other ashrams and hundreds of Siddha Yoga Meditation centers were established throughout the world.

In 1982, shortly before his death, Swami Muktananda designated Swami Chidvilasananda his successor. She had been his disciple since early childhood and had traveled with him since 1973, translating into English his writings, his lectures, and the many informal exchanges he had with his devotees. An advanced spiritual seeker from an early age, with a great longing for God, she became an exemplary disciple. She was guided meticulously in her sadhana by her Guru, who carefully prepared her to succeed him as Guru. In early May of 1982, Swami Chidvilasananda took formal vows of monkhood, and later that month Swami Muktananda bequeathed to her the power and authority of the Siddha lineage, the same spiritual legacy that his Guru had passed on to him. Since that time, Gurumayi, as she is widely known, has given Shaktipat and taught the practices of Siddha Yoga to ever-increasing numbers of seekers, introducing them to Swami Muktananda's message:

> *Meditate on your Self.*
> *Honor your Self.*
> *Worship your Self.*
> *Understand your own Self.*
> *God dwells within you as you.*

INTRODUCTION

The book you are about to read is a classic of spiritual literature. To understand its importance, we must realize that for
centuries the subject of Kundalini has been shrouded in mystery, hedged around by misinformation, and guarded by the
strictest secrecy. This knowledge was so well hidden, in fact,
that when Swami Muktananda received Kundalini awakening from his own Master, Bhagawan Nityananda, and began
experiencing its effects, he had no idea what was happening
to him. He wrote his first great work, the spiritual autobiog-
raphy *Play of Consciousness*, to prevent his own students
from running into the same confusion, and to help them
understand the process unfolding within them.

The experience of Kundalini awakening is incomparable. It is often described as a rebirth, since the deep transformation that occurs can make us feel as if we had been
catapulted into a new world. My own initial experience was
like this. In 1973, three days after my arrival in Swami
Muktananda's ashram in Ganeshpuri, near Bombay, India, I
was sweeping leaves from one of the garden paths. I looked
up and saw Baba coming down the path toward me with a
small group of men. I then watched him pick a leaf from a
eucalyptus tree and examine it with great interest. I stood
aside to let him and the others pass, but to my astonishment,

he stopped right in front of me and handed this leaf to me. He then continued down the path.

Still holding on to the leaf, I entered the temple of the ashram to attend the afternoon chant. I was a little early that day. As I sat waiting for the chant to begin, an incredibly loud explosion occurred right above the top of my head. It sounded like a sonic boom. At the same time, another explosion took place in my chest as though someone had stuck a stick of dynamite into granite. A whole inner world opened up within me. Incredibly powerful waves of love began to surge up inside me. But they were completely unlike any other kind of love I had ever known. This love was completely pure, unconditional, and unbelievably powerful. I remember thinking that this must be what they call divine love. I had read about it in the works of the Spanish mystics years before. The experience was so intense that I started to cry. And I kept crying on and off for two weeks — which was the period of time it took me to adjust to the new state in which I found myself. That state — those waves of divine love surging up inside me — lasted twenty-four hours a day, without interruption, for a year and a half, after which they became sporadic. But though the love has become milder, it has never left.

Whether Shaktipat comes to us dramatically like a sonic boom or very quietly and subtly, as it does to many people, the awakened Kundalini totally transforms our outlook and our experience of ourselves. This is why for so many centuries, in nearly every culture and tradition, Kundalini has been known and revered, for in this mighty power lies the secret of direct spiritual experience, the lifeblood of true religion. Its unfolding has produced the great mystics and men of genius who have flourished in every age. Yet it is not the exclusive property of only a few. Kundalini exists in every human being, though usually in a dormant form. As one ancient Christian text describes it, "In every human being dwells an infinite power, the root of the universe. That infinite power exists in two modes: one actual, the other potential. This infinite power exists in a latent condition in everyone."[1] Once it is awakened, our spiritual evolution is assured.

In the spiritual traditions of many so-called "primitive" peoples of Africa, Australia, and America, Kundalini is recognized as the evolutionary energy which leads man back to his divine source. The Hopi Indians of the southwestern United States are an example. According to the Hopi belief, the first people understood that "the living body of man and the living body of the earth were constructed in the same way. Through each ran an axis, man's axis being the backbone, the vertebral column, which controlled the equilibrium of his movements and his functions. Along this axis were several vibratory centers which echoed the primordial sound of life through the universe or sounded a warning if anything went wrong."[2]

These centers, of course, correspond to the *chakras* described in Kundalini Yoga. In descending order, the Hopis describe them as being located at the top of the head ("the open door" through which man received his life and communicated with his Creator), the brain, the throat, the heart, and under the navel. The two lower chakras referred to in yogic literature, the center at the root of the reproductive organ and the center at the base of the spine, are not mentioned in the Hopi tradition.

According to the Hopis, "Man is created perfect in the image of his Creator. Then after closing the door (at the top of the head) and falling from grace into the uninhibited expression of his own human will, he begins his slow climb back upward . . . With this turn man rises upward, bringing into predominant function each of the higher centers. The door at the crown of the head then opens, and he merges into the wholeness of all Creation, whence he sprang."[3]

Even though knowledge of Kundalini is part of so many traditions, in Western society it was known for a long time only in esoteric circles. Nowadays, understanding of this powerful spiritual force is becoming more widely disseminated, and Western thinkers have become increasingly aware of the vital role Kundalini plays in the evolution of a human being. Nonetheless, it is only when we begin to recognize that our true human potential goes far beyond leading successful personal and professional lives, that we realize the enormous importance of Kundalini awakening. Very few people realize that it is possible to live constantly in a state of totally expanded awareness and joy which we achieve when we become one with the Divine. It is only when Kundalini is awakened that we can begin to experience the infinite freedom of a human being.

A few years ago, Gurumayi Chidvilasananda was visiting Mexico City. A woman approached at the end of one of the evening programs and told Gurumayi that she had "fainted" during the short session of meditation following Gurumayi's talk. The surprising thing, the woman said, was that when she regained her normal consciousness, she understood for the first time in her life that she was absolutely free. Being brand-new to yoga, she was unfamiliar with its terminology, and did not realize that she had not fainted at all, but had entered briefly into a state of *samādhi*, union with the Divine. That mere glimpse of samadhi was enough to remove her mental and emotional limitations for a while, releasing the subtle bonds that keep our awareness of ourselves confined to the body and personality. This profound experience had happened as a result of simply spending a few hours in Gurumayi's presence. Such experiences do occur in the presence of a great *presence of a great master*

Master like Gurumayi. It is a sure sign that the Kundalini energy is being activated.

The scriptures agree that the easiest and safest way to awaken Kundalini is through the grace of a fully realized Master, or Guru. As Baba points out in this book, the awakening and unfolding of Kundalini is the specific function of *the Guru* the Guru. He once wrote, "Only a doctor is qualified to give medicine, a lawyer to practice law, a teacher to teach. Similarly, only a Guru can activate Kundalini." An aphorism of the Kundalini tradition says, "A Guru should be enlightened, he should pierce all the (inner) blocks, and he should transmit and control the Shakti (spiritual energy)."

The role of the Guru in awakening Kundalini is explained very clearly in the ancient philosophical texts of Kashmir Shaivism. One of the most important and comprehensive philosophies of India, Kashmir Shaivism teaches that the entire universe is an expansion of God and demonstrates how a human being can realize his identity with that all-pervasive divine Principle. According to Shaivite texts, the Supreme Reality performs five cosmic *functions* functions: creation, maintenance, and dissolution of the universe, concealment of the true nature of this world, and the bestowal of grace, through which human beings are enabled to realize the truth about themselves and the universe. Shaivism describes the Guru as the embodiment of God's fifth cosmic function, that of grace-bestowal. As the *Shiva Sūtra Vimarshini*, one of the basic texts of Shaivism states, *gururvā pārameshvarī anugrāhikā shaktih*, "The Guru is the grace-bestowing power of God."

The human Guru is, in short, a vehicle for this fifth cosmic process, the descent of grace. Because he has merged his individual awareness into the Divine, the Guru can serve as a pure vessel through which its pure energy flows. It is this energy which awakens and guides the Kundalini, and it is this same infinite power which creates the world, so it can take any form. This is why so many people who have a spiritual bond with a great Master have experienced that Master's presence even when he or she is physically far away. A Siddha Guru, a perfected Master, cannot be confined by limited notions of time and space, and the stories about this are legion.

Several years ago, during an introductory program in the Siddha Yoga ashram in Boston, a video was shown of Swami Muktananda giving a talk. In the video, Baba's translator was the young woman who became Gurumayi. Suddenly, a man in the audience burst into tears for no apparent reason and hurried out of the room. The swami in charge of the program followed him to see what was the matter.

The man told him an incredible story. When he was five years old, he had an unforgettable dream. A car was parked in front of his house with its back door open. Inside, in a haze of blue light, sat a beautiful woman. She beckoned to the little boy, who got into the car and sat on her lap. She put her arms around him, and he was overcome by a deep peace and a feeling of being totally cared for. Soon, in the dream, the boy's father came out to the car and told him, "It's time to go." The little boy refused, protesting that he never wanted to leave her. However, the woman said gently, "You must go now, but don't worry — I will come back."

From that day on, his life became a search to regain that feeling of deep contentment and well-being, and especially the presence that had inspired it. Now, well into his middle years, he had begun to doubt that he would ever again encounter the extraordinary depth of peace he had experienced in that great presence.

That evening, when Gurumayi's face came on the screen, he recognized her immediately as the woman in his childhood dream. Most mysterious of all is that when the man had this dream, Gurumayi had not yet been born.

The process by which the Guru awakens Kundalini is called Shaktipat — the transmission of divine energy. However, it is not enough for the Guru to awaken Kundalini; the Guru also controls and regulates the process, helping to remove all the blocks and obstacles in the disciple's path until the disciple attains the ultimate realization of the Self. Being one with the inner energy, the Guru can accomplish this on a subtle level, from within.

The experience of one of Baba Muktananda's students illustrates how subtly this process can work. When Baba was in Miami Beach during his third world tour, a young Australian man approached him with a problem: he was unable to meditate deeply because of intense fear. As soon as he reached a certain stage in meditation, he would become afraid of losing himself, which triggered in him a deep-rooted fear of death.

Baba, in a few words, reassured him that there was nothing to fear and told him to keep meditating. Several days later, as the young man was sitting in the meditation hall, he turned within and was gripped by this familiar sensation of terror. This time, though, he suddenly found himself outside his physical body, observing it from a distance of a few feet. An inner voice told him, "Do you see that there's nothing to be afraid of? What you are, in essence, has nothing to do with the body and can never die."

He then returned to his physical body and the voice continued, "There's no reason to be afraid. Let's try it again."

The same phenomenon occurred a number of times for several more days during meditation. By this time, the young man had lost his former fear of death and was able to plunge to a deep level of meditation.

In this book, Baba describes some of the extraordinary

experiences which follow Shaktipat as the awakened Kundalini begins to purify the whole system. Since everyone's temperament and degree of preparation is different, everyone initially reacts to Shaktipat in his or her own way. No two individuals receive the Shakti identically. Nevertheless, no matter what form it takes, the awakened Shakti persistently moves us toward higher and more intoxicating levels of reality, until finally we merge into the bliss of the Self. This process is gradual and may seem slow at times, but it is constant, and absolutely unfailing.

In the early days after I received Shaktipat from Baba, I would occasionally have very powerful experiences of the Shakti in meditation. But my daily meditations were not nearly as intense and dramatic as I felt they should be. My mind was still very active, and different mundane issues would often come up when I sat to meditate. I felt very frustrated about this. One morning, in meditation, I had a clear vision of a deep well. I was standing beside it. I could not get into the well because its opening was covered with debris — mud, dirt, leaves, boards, and tree branches. The symbolism of this was very clear to me. I saw that the reason I couldn't go very deep in meditation was because of the mental and emotional debris which I had accumulated inside over many years. At the same time, I also understood that the process Baba had awakened in me would gradually remove all that rubbish. I just had to keep doing the practices which nourish Kundalini, and be patient.

I forgot all about the experience. Ten years passed, and Gurumayi Chidvilasananda became the Guru. One morning in meditation, I found myself at the bottom of the selfsame well. I recognized it instantly. I looked up and saw that enough of the debris had been removed to allow me to get inside. I found myself in a state of absolute ecstasy. All my barriers and limitations were gone. I was completely free. But

I also understood that I couldn't stay at the bottom of the well until the rest of the debris had been removed.

Then I became aware of a presence beside me. I recognized it as the Guru principle, that principle of grace which had been clothed in Baba's physical form for so many years, and which was now embodied in Gurumayi. I realized that it was this Guru principle, working through Kundalini, which had removed the debris from the well, very gradually, day by day.

This is how Kundalini works. Bit by bit, as it moves through the subtle system, blocks are removed, addictions fall away, one's life is set in order. Ultimately, the experience of the Self becomes constant.

Abhinavagupta, a great sage of Kashmir Shaivism, wrote in the tenth century:

adarshe malarahite yadvadvadanam vibhāti tadvadayam
shivashāktipātavimale dhitattve bhāti bharūpah

> Just as a face clearly appears in a spotless mirror,
> in the same way, the Self shines in all its splendor in
> the mind purified by Shaktipat.

Fortunately, this is as true today as it was then. Through the perfected Masters, the power of grace will always flow to those who truly seek it. Such a Master was Swami Muktananda, and such is Gurumayi Chidvilasananda. May their grace, and the grace of the supreme Kundalini, enlighten the minds of all who read this book.

Swami Kripananda
South Fallsburg, New York
December, 1993

Unimaginable the light in the eye!

Indescribable the ring in the ear!

Incomparable the taste on the tongue!

Immeasurable the peace of the inconceivable sushumnā nādī!

Everywhere you will find Him:

In the tiniest particles of dust,

In the hard wood, or a tender blade of grass.

He is everywhere!

The subtle, the imperishable, the unchanging Lord!

— Allama Prabhu

KUNDALINI:
THE SECRET OF LIFE

We live our entire lives with the hope of attaining happiness. Everything we do, we do for the sake of happiness. We get married not for the sake of a wife or a husband but for the sake of happiness. We have children not for their sake but for the sake of our own happiness. We pursue different arts and skills only for the sake of our own happiness.

It is not surprising that this should be so, because happiness is our true nature. Our inner Self is the embodiment of happiness. The Upanishads say that this entire universe is created out of the bliss of God, that it arises from bliss, lives in bliss, and in the end, merges in bliss. So, this bliss, which comes from God, is our birthright. However, we haven't found the real abode of bliss. We haven't learned how to obtain it, and for this reason we remain unhappy.

The closer we get to the inner Self, the more happiness we experience. Often we get a taste of this inner happiness in our ordinary activities. When we wake up from sleep, our minds are completely still for a moment, and we experience that inner contentment. After we have eaten a good meal, we turn within, and for a moment we feel that satisfaction. When we meet friends after a long time and embrace one another, we close our eyes, and turn within,

1

and for a moment we experience that joy. Happiness is present in our life. Yet, because we think happiness comes from outside, we constantly lose touch with it.

Happiness lies inside, and to attain it, we need to turn within. The inner Self is filled with bliss. It is to experience the Self, to come close to the Self, that we practice yoga and meditation.

We badly need knowledge of the Self. It is because we lack this knowledge, which is the knowledge of true humanity, that so many terrible things are happening in the world. It is because we have forgotten the principles of humanity that there is hatred between countries, that there is hatred between people, that violence is increasing everywhere. To attain humanity again, we will have to know who we really are; we will have to realize our own Self. If we don't respect ourselves, how can we respect others? Therefore, first of all, we should know the Self.

Within every human being lies a divine energy called Kundalini. This energy has two aspects: one manifests this worldly existence, and the other leads us to the highest truth. The mundane aspect of this energy is functioning perfectly, but the inner aspect is dormant, sleeping. When the inner Kundalini energy is awakened, it sets off different processes of yoga within us, and leads us to the state of the Self. This is why there is no knowledge more important than the knowledge of Kundalini.

THE NATURE OF KUNDALINI

Almost every tradition speaks of Kundalini in one form or another and describes Kundalini in its own way. In Japanese it is called *ki*; in Chinese, *chi*; the scriptures of Christianity call it the Holy Spirit. What is that Kundalini? It is the power of the Self, the power of Consciousness.

Kundalini is Shakti, supreme energy, whom the sages of India worship as the Mother of the universe. Shakti is the consort of Shiva. She is the active aspect of the formless, attributeless Absolute. People who follow the tradition of bliss call Her Ānanda. *Yogis* make Her the goal of their yoga. Devotees sing Her name with love, and She becomes the object of their love. Enlightened people of knowledge perceive Her in all the forms and objects in the universe, and seeing everything as one in That, they merge in That. There is nothing higher, nothing greater, nothing more sublime and beautiful than Shakti. Dwelling within the center of the heart, She shines with all the colors of the morning sun, and when She is awakened within us, we can see Her there, blazing in all Her effulgence.

What is the nature of this Shakti? She is the supreme creative power of the Absolute Being. Just as heat, which has the power to burn, is not different from fire, Shakti, which has the power to create this universe, is identical with

Parabrahman, the supreme Absolute. She is Brahman in the form of sound, the sound vibration of the Absolute, which manifested the universe. In mantras She is of the form of *mātrikā*, the letters, and in words She is of the form of knowledge. All letters are composed by Her; it is She who brings sound, language, and the alphabet into existence. So, She is alive in all the letters of the alphabet, from beginning to end.

The principal scripture of Kashmir Shaivism, the *Shiva Sūtras*, states: *ichhā shaktir umā kumāri*, "She is the willpower of God, the ever-young maiden called Uma."[4] She is called ever-young because She is always playing; Her play is the creation, sustenance, and dissolution of this world.

Another name for Kundalini is Chiti, universal Consciousness. The first aphorism of the *Pratyabhijñā-hridayam*, another of the principal scriptures of Shaivism, describes Her, saying: *chitih svatantrā vishva siddhi hetuh*, "Universal Consciousness creates this universe by Her own free will." Chiti is supremely independent. No one compels Her to create this universe; She does it on Her own, in supreme freedom, without depending on anything outside. Moreover, as the second aphorism states: *svecchayā svabhittau vishvam unmīlayati*, "She unfolds this universe upon Her own screen."

This universe is manifold. There are so many different things in this universe that we can never know them all, and every atom of this world is filled with Chiti. Everything we know is Chiti. A farmer sows different things in a field — chilis and sugarcane and lemon trees — and when he irrigates the field he has the same water feeding different plants. When the water goes into the lemon tree, it takes on the quality of lemon and becomes sour, and when it goes into the chili, it becomes hot. But even though it manifests in all these different forms, the soil is the same, the water is the same, the farmer is the same. In the same way, Chiti, the cosmic energy, becomes this manifold universe. She doesn't create this universe the way a human being builds a house, using different kinds of materials and remaining different from those materials. She creates the universe out of Her own being, and it is She Herself who becomes this universe. She becomes all the elements of the universe and enters into all the different forms that we see around us. She becomes the sun, the moon, the stars, and fire to illuminate the cosmos which She creates. She becomes *prāna*, the vital force, to keep all creatures, including humans and birds, alive; it is She who, to quench our thirst, becomes water. To satisfy our hunger, She becomes food. Whatever we see or don't see, whatever exists, right from the earth to the sky, is nothing but Chiti, nothing but Kundalini. It is that supreme energy which moves and animates all creatures, from the elephant to the tiniest ant. She enters each and every creature and thing that She creates, yet never loses Her identity or Her immaculate purity.

This divine power is the power of our own Self. Though we talk about awakening the Kundalini, the truth is that everyone's Kundalini is already awake. Just as She has created the external universe and dwells within it, She has created this human body and pervades it from head to toe. Dwelling at the center of the universe, She holds it together and maintains it. In the same way, dwelling at the center of the body, in the *mūlādhāra chakra* at the base of the spine, She controls and maintains our whole physiological system, through its network of 720 million *nādīs*.

Kundalini is the support of our lives; it is She who makes everything work in our bodies. When Her flow is external, Kundalini functions through the mind and senses and provides the motive power for all our activities. She is at the root of all the senses of perception and organs of action, and She makes each one work according to its nature. Moreover, it is She who hears through our ears, sees through our eyes, and tastes through our tongue. She makes the mind think, the intellect decide and discriminate, and the imagination fantasize. It is She who brings the breath in and out and makes the heart beat. It is the inner aspect of Kundalini which has to be awakened. Kundalini in Her outer aspect is all-pervasive, and that is why even though She is functioning inside us, we don't perceive Her. Only through subtle understanding can we come to know Her; without understanding, we cannot find Her. This understanding arises when the inner Kundalini becomes active. Being all-pervasive, Kundalini is the witness of everything, the knower of everything that can be known. We cannot know Her, but She can know Herself. The sun illuminates the world and also illuminates itself, and in the same way the effulgent Kundalini, which illuminates the mind, the intellect, the senses and their objects, also illuminates Herself and makes Herself known.

THE NEED TO AWAKEN KUNDALINI

The awakening of the inner Kundalini is the true beginning of the spiritual journey. Just as when She is directed outward, Kundalini enables us to explore the outer world, when Her inner aspect is activated, we are able to experience the inner, spiritual world. The scriptures say that as long as the inner Kundalini is sleeping, it doesn't matter how many austerities we follow, how much yoga we practice, or how many mantras we repeat, we will never realize our identity with our inner Self. We will never know our own divinity, or understand God, or experience the all-pervasiveness of Consciousness. In our present state, we identify ourselves with this body which has a certain size and shape. We are not aware that we are all-pervasive. It is only when the Kundalini is awakened that we become aware of our true nature, of our greatness, of the fact that not only do we belong to God but we *are* God. If our Shakti hasn't been awakened, then even if God were to take a form and appear before us, we wouldn't be able to know Him or experience Him as He truly is. Lord Krishna was Arjuna's charioteer. He was with Arjuna constantly, but Arjuna didn't derive any benefit from His company. It was only when the Lord bestowed His grace upon Arjuna and awakened his inner Shakti that Arjuna was really able to know Him.

It is very difficult to know the supreme Principle. Even though It does everything, It does not identify Itself as the doer. A verse in the *Shiva Mahimnah Stotram* says, "How can I describe You when You are beyond the mind, body, and senses?" When the Self is limitless, unborn, and eternal, how can It be known? Only through the medium of Shakti can we gain entry to the Self. Shakti is the pathway to God. Shakti is the face of Shiva. When we look at someone's face we know who he is; and in the same way, when we perceive the Shakti working within, we come to know God.

That is why it is essential to awaken the inner Kundalini Shakti. According to Shaivism, when one acquires the strength of Kundalini, one expands infinitely, and then one assimilates this whole universe; one is able to see the whole universe within one's Self. One no longer remains a limited, bound creature; one achieves total union with God. One merges with Shiva and becomes Shiva.

THE AWAKENING OF KUNDALINI

Although Kundalini pervades the human body, She has a special abode at the center of the body, in the muladhara chakra at the base of the spine. In fact, there are three kinds of Kundalini within the body — Prana Kundalini, Chit Kundalini and Para Kundalini — each of which has a different location.* Kundalini can be awakened at all three locations; however, it is at muladhara that She is usually awakened. The word *mūla* means "root," and *adhāra* means "support." According to the yogic scriptures, this root is three inches long, and within it the Shakti resides in a subtle form, coiled three and one-half times; this is why She is known as Kundalini, "the coiled one." When She is awakened, She uncoils and begins to journey upwards toward the abode of Shiva in the *sahasrāra*.

There are several ways in which the Kundalini Shakti can be awakened. She can be aroused through intense devotion to God, through repetition of mantra, or through the practice of various yogic exercises. In rare cases, an aspirant can even experience a spontaneous awakening due to the merit accumulated from *sādhanā*, spiritual practices, performed in past births. Different modes of awakening the

---

*The knowledge about these three Kundalinis, and their locations, can only be received from the Guru.

9

Kundalini have been described in the scriptures. However, the easiest and best method is through Shaktipat from the Guru, when the Guru directly transmits his own divine Shakti into the disciple. It is the divine function of the Guru to awaken the dormant Shakti; when the Guru transmits his power into a disciple, the inner aspect of Kundalini is automatically activated and set into operation.

Shaktipat is a great and divine science. It is the secret initiation of the greatest sages and has been passed on from Guru to disciple from the beginning of time.

The tradition of initiation exists in every path and in every sect. However, the true initiation is Shaktipat, the inner awakening by which the disciple can have a super-conscious vision of the Absolute, and through which, in time, he comes to experience his identity with God.

THE GURU

Only that Guru can give Shaktipat who has received Shaktipat from his own Guru and whose Kundalini has fully unfolded, establishing him permanently in the place of perfection within, which is the source of the Shakti. The scriptures say: *gururvā pārameshvarī anugrāhikā shaktih,* "The Guru is the grace-bestowing power of God." [5] A true Guru, then, is one who can bestow divine grace on a disciple through Shaktipat, who can awaken the three aspects of Kundalini, who can pierce all the blocks in the disciple's spiritual centers, and who can still the disciple's wandering mind and help him find peace within himself. Such a Guru knows the scriptures thoroughly and is adept at explaining the mysteries of scriptural truths. He can command and wield authority and can control the workings of the Shakti in a disciple.

The entire body of such a Guru has become permeated with Shakti. In fact, the Guru becomes the embodiment of Shakti to such an extent that the hat he wears, his clothes, and the mat on which he sits become permeated with it, and just by touching them, a disciple can receive Shakti.

The philosopher Amir Khusrau received knowledge of the Truth from the shoes of the great Sufi saint Nizamuddin.

11

The poet-saint Kabir received his own awakening from the unintended touch of his Guru's sandals. If one is worthy, if one has great love and faith in the Guru, one receives the Guru's Shakti very easily.

There is another story which illustrates this. In Benares, there lived a great saint called Ravidas, who was a cobbler. Many people used to come to him, and one of these was the prime minister of that state. When the prime minister met Ravidas he experienced peace and contentment within himself, and he went back to the palace and told the king, "You should go to see the saint Ravidas. You will receive some joy from him."

In India, in those days, the caste system was prevalent. When the king heard that Ravidas was a cobbler, he didn't know how he could go and see him. But one day there was a fair, and while all the people of the city were at the fair, the king put on a disguise and went to the house of Ravidas.

"O Saint," said the king, "I lack peace. Even though I have so much outer wealth, inside I am empty."

Ravidas was an omniscient being, so he knew everything that was going on inside the king's mind. In India, a cobbler keeps a pot of stone which holds the water in which he dips leather. Ravidas dipped a cup in that water and told the king to drink it. Now, the king had been hesitant before, but when the saint gave him the dirty water to drink, he became completely disgusted. He turned his back to the saint, and instead of drinking the water, he poured it down his shirt. Then he left, went back to the palace, and called the royal washerman.

"My shirt has become very dirty," he said. "Take it and wash it well."

The washerman was amazed to see the king's shirt in such condition. He made inquiries and found out that the

king had gone to Ravidas's house, that Ravidas had given
him the cup of water to drink, and that the king had
poured the water on the shirt. The washerman called his
daughter and told her what had happened. Then he gave
her the shirt and told her to wash it.

The daughter was very intelligent. She took the shirt
and sucked all the stains out of it, then cleaned it and gave
it back to her father. That evening, when her work was
over, she became absorbed in meditation on the Self. In
time, she became a very great saint, and many people
began to come to see her from different places. The prime
minister also visited her. He went to the king and told him
about the girl. He said to the king, "I don't see any change
in you. You are still worried and unhappy. Why don't you
go to see that girl?"

So the king went to the girl and prayed to her, "I am
very unhappy, and I lack peace. Please give me some happiness and peace."

"O Your Majesty," she said, "everything I have
attained, I attained from sucking the stains on the shirt
you gave me to wash. Everything I got, I got from you! So
what can I give you now?"

This is the value of the Guru's *prasād*. A true Guru
doesn't have to give initiation deliberately. Simply by
spending some time with such a Guru or in the environ-
ment permeated by his Shakti, one can receive his initiation spontaneously. The power of a great saint's company
is such that it affects everyone who comes in contact
with him.

Lord Gauranga Mahaprabhu was a great ecstatic being
who used to dance constantly, singing, *Hare Rāma Hare
Krishna*. Once, a millionaire became irritated with him and
sent two of his most beautiful concubines to seduce him.
Gauranga was sitting beside the road, chanting and swaying

in ecstasy when the concubines came up beside him. They sat down beside him, and as they listened to him his Shakti passed into them, and both the prostitutes became filled with love for God. They became Gauranga's followers and spent the rest of their lives in devotion.

How the Shakti Is Awakened

There are four ways in which the Guru deliberately awakens the Shakti: by touch, word, look, and thought. The first method is initiation through touch, called *sparsha dīkshā*. There are three main places that the Guru touches: one is in the space between the eyebrows at the *ājñā* chakra, another place is in the heart, and the third place is the muladhara, at the base of the spine. It was through his touch that Shri Ramakrishna gave Vivekananda an instantaneous experience of divinity.

The second method of initiation is through word, or mantra diksha, in which the Guru's Shakti enters the disciple by means of the mantra. The Guru who gives this mantra has repeated it himself for a long time during the course of his sadhana, has realized the power of the mantra, and is able to charge it with a living conscious force. His whole being is saturated with the mantra. When the Guru has made his mantra divine and alive, that mantra is then known as a *chaitanya*, or conscious, mantra. This mantra is perfect; it brings liberation, as well as bestowing all types of powers. Through constant repetition of the mantra, the Kundalini is awakened. If the Guru whispers the mantra directly into a seeker's ear, then the Kundalini may be immediately awakened.

When one practices the *prāna* mantra, *So'ham*, becoming aware of the syllables *ham* and *sa* which come in and go out with the breath, the Shakti awakens very quickly.

look

The third method is called *drik* diksha, initiation through a look. One who gives this initiation should have an inward look. If you look at the pictures of the great saints, you will see that their eyes are directed inward, at the inner Self. Even though the eyes of such a being are open and appear to be looking outward, actually his attention is fixed within his own being. So, only one who is permanently established in the inward look can give initiation through the eyes.

thought

The fourth way is initiation by thought, called *manasa* diksha, in which the Guru just thinks about it and the person gets initiated.

When there is an instantaneous experience of the Supreme Reality through either the touch, word, look, or thought of the Guru, this initiation is called *shambhavi* diksha. This is the great initiation. However, few people have the strength to bear the force of the impact of such an initiation.

Not everybody receives the same effect of Shaktipat. Shaktipat is of three degrees: mild, medium, and intense. These are further divided into nine subcategories each, making twenty-seven ways in which one can receive Shaktipat. Still, the Shakti is one. Only one Shakti is transmitted in Shaktipat; however, people are of different capacities or temperaments. Each person receives Shaktipat according to his nature, his actions, and the accumulation of his sins and virtues. The Kundalini dwells in everyone; therefore, this energy can be awakened in everyone, but it depends entirely on one's faith, devotion, and desire for the awakening. The Guru gives Shakti to whomever takes it. There is no such thing as giving it to one and denying it to another. If one asks to whom the sun gives heat, the answer is, to whomever stands in front of it. If one stays indoors, one will remain cold. So, anyone can receive Shakti from the Guru. It is just that some people receive it sooner, while for others it comes later.

Once a woman from Sweden came to our ashram and stayed for eight days. At the end of that time she came to me and complained that she hadn't received anything, and that she was going home. "Very good," I told her. "You can go." She left the ashram and went to Bombay. Two days later, she got on a plane for Sweden. On the plane, the Shakti grabbed her. She began doing spontaneous *prāṇāyāma* — breath-control exercises. When she got home, she wrote me a letter telling me what had happened. That is how the Shakti is. You never know when it will become active. Once you have received the grace of the Guru, it will never go to waste. Lifetime after lifetime it will keep pursuing you, waiting for the time when it can begin to work.

Nonetheless, if you want the Shakti to work with its full power, you have to take care of it. This Shakti creates a new life. After receiving it, you should be able to digest it. You should not lose it or throw it away by undisciplined living or by neglecting your sadhana. Instead, you should try to understand it and enhance it. Meditation, chanting, the repetition of the mantra, faith, and love for the Guru, a pure and regular life, all make the Shakti increase. Generally speaking, once you have received the Shakti, love for God and the desire for sadhana begin to arise in you on their own. The Shakti itself leads you on the proper path.

SIDDHA YOGA

Just as a seed contains a whole tree in potential form, Kundalini contains all the different forms of yoga, and when She is awakened through the grace of the Guru, She makes all yogas take place within you spontaneously. The process which begins when you receive Shaktipat is called Siddha Yoga, the "perfect yoga," or Maha Yoga, the "great yoga." The path of Siddha Yoga is the path which has been trodden by great saints. It has a long and great lineage and has existed since the Creation. This yoga bears its fruit immediately. Now, in this very lifetime, wherever you happen to be, the power of Kundalini allows you to realize the truth of the Self, through which spiritual and worldly life merge into one.

Siddha Yoga is called Maha Yoga because it encompasses all other yogas. There are many kinds of yogas: hatha yoga, the practice of physical exercises; *bhakti* yoga, the path of love; *rāja* yoga, which is attained through meditation; mantra yoga; *laya* yoga; *jñāna* yoga and many others. When Kundalini is awakened, all these other yogas take place automatically. You don't have to make any effort to practice them; they come to you on their own.

For instance, after Shaktipat, one may experience involuntary movements of the body, such as shaking and movements of the arms and legs. The head may even begin to rotate violently. One may automatically perform various yogic *āsanas*, *mudrās*, *bandhas* and different kinds of pranayama, which are all parts of hatha yoga. All these physical movements, called *kriyās*, are spontaneous movements of the Kundalini through the body in order to bring about purification. When we practice exercises on the basis of our limited understanding, we cannot possibly know which particular asanas, mudras, bandhas and pranayamas are good for us. For example, *sarvāngāsana* may be the position which is the best suited for my constitution, but I may be practicing *shīrshāsana*, which isn't good for me at all, and if I go on practicing it, I may get a brain disease instead of acquiring mastery of yoga. But when these movements occur spontaneously, you automatically perform only those postures which are necessary and appropriate.

Kundalini is all-knowing. She knows our past and our future, and She knows what is suited to us and what is not.

Just as one experiences the movements of hatha yoga, other yogas also take place. Love arises, along with the ecstatic feeling of devotion which belongs to bhakti yoga. One attains spontaneous knowledge, as in jnana yoga, and the capacity for detachment in action, which belongs to karma yoga. You may hear inner sounds, perceive divine tastes and smells, or have visions of various lights, gods and goddesses, saints, holy rivers and mountains, and even distant worlds, as in laya yoga. You may begin spontaneously to recite mantras in Sanskrit and other languages, to sing, to roar like a lion, hiss like a snake, chirp like a bird, or make various other sounds. You may be inspired to compose beautiful poetry. You develop a great interest in chanting, in repeating the name of God, and in reading the scriptures. These manifestations correspond to mantra yoga.

When the awakened Kundalini rises through the central channel, She pierces the six chakras, or spiritual centers, the three knots (*brahmagranthi, vishnugranthi* and *rudragranthi*), and finally brings about the *samādhi* state, the state of equality-awareness, establishing the disciple permanently in the topmost spiritual center, the sahasrara, where he becomes one with Lord Shiva. This manifestation of the Kundalini corresponds to raja yoga and culminates in the ultimate realization of God within oneself. In this way, Siddha Yoga is very easy, very natural. There are many paths through which you attain the final goal with great effort and difficulty, but in Siddha Yoga you attain it very naturally and spontaneously. The samadhi that follows Kundalini awakening is not the kind of samadhi which makes you inert. It is a conscious samadhi; it makes you more alert, more aware. This state has been called in the *Shiva Sūtras: lokānandah samādhisukham,* "The bliss of the world is the ecstasy of samadhi."[6] In this state one recognizes the presence of God in everything. The whole purpose of Kundalini awakening is to attain this natural samadhi while continuing to function in the world.

THE CENTRAL CHANNEL

This body may appear from the outside to be made simply *nadis* of flesh and blood, but that's not really what it is. This body is also made of nadis, or channels. Just as if you open the front of a car and look inside, you will see many wires, in the same way, within the body you find many nadis. These nadis perform different functions. Some are channels for blood, some for wind, some for prana, and so on. Among the 720 million nadis which make up this body, there are one hundred which are important, which support all the other nadis. Among these nadis are ten which control the one hundred; and these ten nadis are supported by three nadis which are of the highest importance: the *idā*, the *pingalā*, and the *sushumnā*.

Everyone's ida and pingala nadis are active, because when one inhales and exhales, the breath comes in and goes out through these nadis. However, most people are unaware of the sushumna nadi, which is the most significant of the 720 million nadis. The sushumna is situated between the ida and pingala in the center of the spinal column. The various activities of life are possible only because of the sushumna. The sushumna controls all the other nadis. It extends in an unbroken line from the muladhara, where the dormant Kundalini lies coiled up, to the sahasrara in the crown of the head, the seat of supreme Shiva. Within the sushumna is a subtle nadi called *chitrinī*, which is the channel for the movement of the Kundalini. The sushumna is also called the *brahma* nadi (the channel of the Absolute), the *samvitti* nadi (the channel of consciousness), the *madhya* nadi (the central channel), or the pathway of the great Kundalini.

Whatever thoughts one has come from this central nadi, and all one's karmas and impressions from many lives are lodged here. All the different states we experience — desire or greed, inspiration or dullness — arise from the sushumna. In the upper region of the sushumna are such qualities as contentment, peace, and knowledge, while in the lower region lie the passions of lust, greed, anger, and all the feelings of insecurity and inadequacy. When your Shakti is awakened, all the past impressions and karmas come out. That is why when you first receive Shaktipat, you sometimes feel very negative or very angry. You shouldn't be afraid when you get into such a state; it happens because the Shakti is expelling all the karmas of countless lives. Sometimes when a person receives Shaktipat, he begins either to laugh for hours on end with joy or to cry for hours with great grief. Sometimes he becomes absorbed in a divine feeling; sometimes he appears mad. One who has knowledge of these things understands that they are different manifestations of the Shakti.

After you receive Shaktipat, meditation starts spontaneously, and at that time, prana and *apāna*, the ingoing and outgoing breath, become balanced, and long *kumbhaka* (retention of breath) begins to take place effortlessly. The prana becomes extremely subtle and moves into the sushumna, and then the sushumna opens up and begins to unfold.

The *Pratyabhijñāhridayam* says: *madhya vikāsāc chidā-*

nanda lābhah, "When the central nadi is unfolded, one experiences the bliss of Consciousness."[7] If the central nadi is not unfolded, a person cannot evolve. The unfolding of the central nadi is the pilgrimage to liberation, the path of Self-realization. If you have received Shakti from the Guru, then the central channel unfolds automatically.

unfolding of sushumnā is the pilgrimage toward liberation

FEARS ABOUT KUNDALINI AWAKENING

Some people say that when the Kundalini is awakened, there is danger that you might go crazy, or that your body might be afflicted with terrible diseases. These fears are unfounded; there are no diseases in the belly of Kundalini. On the contrary, the Kundalini eats up diseases and exudes pure elixir. However, some people do attempt to awaken the Kundalini forcibly, through self-effort, either by means of hatha yogic techniques such as mudras and bandhas, or with their own unusual practices, and anything may happen in such a case. If the Kundalini were not to rise in a proper manner, it might prove to be harmful. A person who tries to bring about this kind of awakening on his own with unusual practices does not succeed in raising his Kundalini, he only succeeds in irritating Her. And if the Kundalini is irritated beyond a certain limit, a person might lose his mental balance, or his body might become weak. But if Kundalini awakens through Guru's grace, spontaneously, and if the processes of Kundalini Yoga are set in motion by the Shakti Herself, such adverse reactions would be impossible, because in the kingdom of Kundalini there is no sickness or mental disease.

Sometimes a seeker may pass through a stage which seems difficult. For instance, a person who has a weak mind or a tendency toward mental sickness may find that as a result of Kundalini awakening he appears to be deluded or crazy for a while. But this is happening to expel the tendency from his system, and there is nothing at all to fear. Occasionally people come to our ashrams who are mentally disturbed, who have lost their reason, and when Kundalini gets awakened in them, She builds a new intellect for them; they get new powers of reasoning.

When Kundalini awakening takes place through grace, it will rise of its own accord and become established where it should be established. Kundalini will take care of Herself, for the Shakti is a conscious and all-knowing power. It is not enough for the Kundalini to be merely awakened, it must rise to the sahasrara and become established there. If one has awakened the Kundalini through self-effort, it is very difficult to lead it upward, because right from the moment the Kundalini is awakened until the moment it finally merges in the sahasrara, the seeker has to depend on yogic practices. But when the Kundalini is awakened by the grace of the Guru, the grace itself will guide it in the correct manner. There is absolutely no danger in such a case.

Those who do manage to awaken the Kundalini without the grace of a Guru do have certain experiences, but they get confused because they do not have the guidance of a perfect Master. They are limited by their previous knowledge, which is inadequate to explain these new experiences, and, therefore, they hesitate to accept many experiences as valid. They doubt the experiences which come to them and to others, not understanding that Kundalini's powers are limitless, and that She can manifest unlimited worlds inside as well as outside. To speak with authority about the workings of Kundalini, one must have practiced Kundalini Yoga under the guidance of a perfected Master. One must have practiced it in a systematic fashion according to scriptural injunctions and must have achieved final perfection.

Many lesser teachers can effect a partial awakening, but the Kundalini soon becomes dormant again, leaving the seeker in an anxious state. A lot of people who met me during my world tours said, "My Kundalini was awakened three years ago, but now it is asleep again." This is what happens when one does not have the grace of a perfected Master, and such an awakening does not serve much purpose. Only a Guru who has received the blessing of the supreme Goddess and his own Guru and who has received the command to perform Shaktipat, can bring about a permanent awakening that can take the seeker to the final goal.

PURIFICATION OF THE BODY AND MIND

Most of us have knowledge only about the physical body. However, the truth is that we do not have only one body but four. They are the gross body, in which we experience the pains and pleasures of the waking state; the subtle body, in which we dream; the causal body, which is the body of deep sleep; and the supracausal body, which is the body of the superconscious or *turīya* state. The Shakti works in all the four bodies. One who meditates systematically will pass through all these bodies successively, and will see in meditation the four lights — red, white, black, and blue — which correspond to them. These lights appear one within the other. The red light is the size of the physical body. The white light is thumb-sized, the black light is the size of a fingertip, while the blue light is the size of a sesame seed.

Prana is the most important element in the body; when the prana leaves the body, it becomes worth only a few pennies. It is Shakti in the form of prana which supports the body, the senses, and the mind. In fact, the entire universe arises from prana. The scriptures say: *prāk samvit prāne parinatā,* "Universal Consciousness evolves into prana,"[8] and *sarvam prāne pratishthitam,* "Everything is established in prana." Although the prana shakti is only one, in order to carry out the different functions of

27

the body in an orderly manner, She takes five forms:
prana, apana, *samāna*, *vyāna* and *udāna*. Prana is the
breath, which comes in and goes out. Apana expels waste
matter from the body. Samana distributes the nourishment of our food to the different places in the body.
Vyana pervades the body as the power of movement
which makes it function. Udana resides in the sushumna
and works upwards.

Often, when Kundalini first becomes active, you
feel heavy-headed and sleepy. This is a result of the
movement of prana, and it is a sure sign that the
Kundalini has been awakened. As Kundalini moves up
through the sushumna, She transforms the body and
makes it fit for spiritual sadhana; it is only after the body
has been purified that the Shakti can work with full
force. The basis of all disease and pain is the impurities
which block the flow of prana in the nadis. These blockages are caused by imbalances and disorders in the three
bodily humors — wind, bile, and phlegm — due to
undisciplined habits of eating and immoderate living. In
order to purify the nadis, Kundalini inspires the various
hatha yogic movements or kriyas, which take place in
the physical body. In the form of prana, She penetrates
all 720 million nadis, consumes all the old decaying flu-
ids, then releases vital energy into them all. As the nadis
become filled with prana, the body becomes rejuvenated
from within. It becomes strong and firm, with all the
suppleness of a child.

Sometimes during this process, latent germs of diseases may be brought to the surface, and as a result, the
person may start to suffer from that disease. However,
this is happening to expel this disease from the system
permanently, and there is nothing to be afraid of. During
the days of my wandering around India, I contracted

chronic dysentery because I was traveling from place to place and eating whatever food was given to me. During one period of my sadhana this intensified so much that I began having forty to fifty stools every day. After a while I lost my strength and could not even get up to go to the toilet. Some of my friends were worried about me, but I wasn't at all frightened. Later this stopped automatically and permanently.

The purification of the nadis is purification of the entire system. The same blockages which cause diseases also give rise to such feelings as aversion, hatred, lethargy, dullness, and greed, and these qualities also disappear when the nadis are washed by Kundalini. When the nadis are cleansed, the mind is purified. The mind is intimately connected to the prana. When the prana becomes uneven, the sense of duality arises, and the mind keeps weaving new webs of thoughts and fantasies. To control the mind, to make it still and even, yogis try to control the breath. This is why they practice so many different kinds of pranayama, or breath control. During the process of Siddha Yoga purification, natural pranayama begins to take place. The prana and apana (the outgoing and incoming breaths) become even, and eventually the breath begins to be retained within. This is called kumbhaka. Shaivism says that to keep controlling your breath is not true kumbhaka. In true kumbhaka, the prana and apana become one. At that point, prana does not go out, nor does apana come in. When the prana stops, the mind becomes still, and you experience supreme tranquility. Great beings are in this state of inner stillness. If you look at the picture of my Guru, Nityananda, you will see that he has a big belly. This is not because he ate too much but because of the inner kumbhaka.

This inner kumbhaka is extremely valuable. The state

of kumbhaka is the state of pure wisdom, pure knowledge.
When spontaneous knowledge takes place, you come to
know the *Hamsa* pranayama. You become aware of the self-
born mantra going on within you, of the syllables *ham* and
sa flowing in and out with the breath. This is the Siddha
mantra, the natural *japa* of perfected beings. It is the
awareness of "I am That," the awareness of your identity
with the Truth.

THE INNER JOURNEY
OF KUNDALINI

Within the sushumna are six chakras, or spiritual centers, which block the pathway of the Kundalini as it rises to the sahasrara. As the Shakti unfolds, all these chakras are pierced. The scriptures explain the different locations of the different chakras: the muladhara, near the anus; the *svādhishthāna*, between the navel and the sexual organ; the *manipūra*, in the navel; the *anāhata*, in the heart; the *vishuddha*, in the throat; and the ajna, in the space between the eyebrows.

These six chakras can be experienced only through yoga and meditation. You cannot discover them by studying anatomy. Modern scientists haven't found a way to register these chakras on their machines, because they are too subtle. However, you begin experiencing them in meditation as the Kundalini moves up the sushumna.

THE HEART

When Kundalini has purified the lower chakras, She rises into the heart. There is a great spiritual center here, and when this center is activated, subtle experiences and inner purification take place, and you begin to experience the different inner worlds.

When Kundalini reaches this level, the heart opens, and waves upon waves of bliss keep arising within. There is a beautiful light in the heart, which one sees in meditation. Moreover, there is a center of pure knowledge there, and when Kundalini begins to work in the heart, knowledge arises in you spontaneously. Different powers such as clairaudience, clairvoyance, and the power of healing come automatically.

I am writing from my own experience, describing experiences which came to me during sadhana, after my Kundalini was awakened through the grace of my Guru. After the awakening of Kundalini, meditation comes spontaneously. There is no need to center the mind because the Kundalini Herself grabs hold of the mind and centers it in whatever place She considers suitable. As you get deeper and deeper into meditation, you have innumerable subtle experiences.

There is a state called *tandrā*, which you spontaneously slip into under the inspiration of Kundalini. In tandra you

have visions of mountains, rivers, deities, saints and even
other worlds. Tandra resembles the state of sleep, but it is
quite different from the dream state. The visions you have
in tandra are not like hallucinations or dreams but are as
real as the sights you see with your physical eyes. Often
you have visions of events in the outer world, which turn
out to be true. In fact, you are able to see the entire universe in the state of tandra while sitting in one place with
closed eyes. At times, you may see the whole system of
nerves, veins, and arteries, and the digestive and elimina-
tive tracts in the body in a multicolored light, which
spreads through all the nadis. You can even see the prana
flowing through them with increasing intensity as the
purification of the body continues.

While meditating in the state of tandra, I visited
many different inner worlds. In meditation I traveled to
the world of the moon, the world of departed spirits, to
heaven and hell, and to the world of the Siddhas, which is
inhabited by great saints and sages of all traditions. After
seeing these worlds, I came to realize that the descriptions
of the different planes of existence which one reads in the
scriptures and in the writings of the ancient sages and yogis
are absolutely true. All these worlds are extremely subtle;
they cannot be seen with the physical eyes.

It is not surprising that one should be able to see so
many worlds, because Consciousness has the ability to create infinite universes. On my second world tour, I met an
astronaut who had visited the moon. I told him that if he
could get into meditation, he would be able to explore
many different inner worlds while sitting in one place with
closed eyes. If you were to travel to the moon by the outer
route, it would take a long time and would be a lot of trou-
ble and expense. But if the inner Shakti unfolds, and you
go within, you can go there in half a second. Though out-

wardly they may be far away, on the inside all these worlds are very close. You can understand this by the example of a shortwave radio. If you move the dial to one side, you get the news of Bombay. If you turn it half an inch, you get the news from New York. If you went on a plane, it would take you fourteen or fifteen hours to get the news, but on the radio it takes not even half a second. In the same way, when Kundalini is awakened, you can travel to these distant worlds in an instant.

There are more subtle experiences which can come to a meditator as the Kundalini rises through the sushumna. Not every meditator will have all these experiences, for experience varies according to one's temperament and the intensity of one's faith and devotion. But everyone who practices meditation under the guidance of a perfect Master will certainly experience some of these things. Through these experiences one's understanding, one's perception, and one's entire being are gradually transformed.

KUNDALINI AWAKENING
IN DAILY LIFE

The awakened Kundalini transforms us on every level of our being, and this means that She will take care of our worldly life as well. When Kundalini is awakened, She transforms our outlook and makes us see the world around us in a new way. What has seemed difficult and frustrating begins to seem enjoyable and full of flavor, and we have new enthusiasm for our activities and pursuits.

Kundalini generates supreme friendliness among people. She makes us able to see each other as divine, to see our husband or wife, our friends and neighbors, our children and parents, as filled with God. She improves our daily life and makes perfect whatever is not perfect in our lives. Where you have deficiencies, She strengthens and fills you. She will make you able to look after your family in a better way and take care of your business or profession more skillfully and intelligently. She improves a student's memory and concentration. She makes an artist a better artist, a doctor a better doctor. Kundalini is the source of poetry, of music, of the power of intuitive reasoning, of the scientist's capacity of invention, of the statesman's ability to administrate. All talents, all inspiration, all creativity lie in the womb of Kundalini, and when She is awakened, She releases great creative powers. There are people who

after this awakening become great poets or compose significant philosophical works. For some, Kundalini takes the
form of Lakshmi, the goddess of wealth, and they come
into a lot of money. In others it takes the form of authority,
and they become great leaders.

The scriptures say, "Where there is liberation, there
are no worldly enjoyments, and where there are worldly
enjoyments, there is no liberation; but when one enjoys
the grace of the supremely lovely Kundalini, worldly
enjoyment and liberation go hand in hand." Kundalini
has created this entire universe and pervades every parti-
cle of it. So it should not surprise you that She should be
able to take care of your worldly life, which is, after all,
Her own creation.

Many of the great saints of the Siddha tradition were
householders, who lived full lives in the world and
attained God while going about their ordinary activities.
Siddha Yoga is not meant only for liberation. It also gives
worldly happiness and fulfills your inner desires. Kundalini
is the wish-fulfilling tree. She will bring you whatever you
want in this world.

THE AJNA CHAKRA

As Kundalini keeps rising, as all the lower chakras are pierced, one's awareness comes to the space between the eyebrows, which is called the ajna chakra. This chakra is also called the seat of the Guru. Ājñā means "command," and the Kundalini will not move past this center without the command of the inner Guru. As the ajna chakra is pierced, you experience the merging state of the mind. The mind becomes very still and one-pointed, and the thoughts which have created disturbances become quiet. This is the beginning of the final stage of sadhana, which leads to the ultimate attainment. After piercing through the ajna chakra, Kundalini rises to the sahasrara.

PURIFICATION OF THE SENSES

On Her journey to the sahasrara, Kundalini passes through all the sense organs, purifying them and investing them with new powers. As long as the chakras of the sense organs are not purified, the senses work in an ordinary manner, but when they are purified, they acquire divine powers and even the physical senses become sharpened and refined. As Kundalini rises to the ocular center, She purifies the eyes through the process called *bindu-bedha*. When She settles in the pupils, the eyes gain a new power, and one can see objects at a great distance. Through the process of bindu-bedha, one is able to see the universe as it really is: a mass of blue light, which sparkles and scintillates all the time and which is not discernible through the physical eyes. This subtle bluish light pervades everywhere; it is just like the tender after-image which persists after someone flashes his camera at you. It is not like a continuous sheet but is made up of particles like tiny sparks, constantly shimmering.

As the Kundalini purifies the sense of touch, one begins to feel thrills of love through every pore and hair of the body. One becomes immersed in the joy of touch.

When Kundalini reaches the center of smell located between the eyebrows, it purifies that, and then one comes into direct contact with the subtle essence of smell.

According to the Indian scriptures, the earth principle springs from this subtle essence of smell, and all our food and plants and flowers trace their scent back to this essence. When Kundalini stabilizes in this center of divine fragrance, such subtle smells are released that one is overwhelmed. No external perfume could surpass this fragrance.

When the Shakti moves to the auditory center, She purifies this through a process known as *karna-bedha*. As this center is purified, you begin to hear the celestial harmonies resounding in the upper spaces in the sahasrara. These inner sounds have been called the music of the spheres. All the outer music is an attempt to approximate these inner harmonies. They cannot be recreated by even the finest musicians or the finest musical instruments.

As one listens to this divine *nāda*, one begins to hear the sound of inner thunder and the *khecharī* mudra takes place, in which the tongue curls upward into the nasal pharynx. This mudra is extremely significant. Yogis work for as long as fifteen years, pulling their tongues out to elongate them and even cutting their tongues with a razor, yet they do not succeed in mastering the khechari mudra. There is a knot in the sushumna, within the cranial region, called the rudragranthi, or knot of Rudra. This knot is opened by the tip of the tongue as it touches it during khechari mudra. Then the awakened Shakti rises to the sahasrara, to unite with Shiva dwelling there. After this, one starts to experience samadhi states and taste the divine nectar.

Just as the rain follows thunder in the atmosphere, the same thing happens in the inner spaces. When the thunder sounds in the inner spaces and khechari mudra takes place, a shower of nectar begins to fall. There is a pool of nectar behind the forehead, and during khechari mudra this nectar is released and drops onto the root of the tongue. When the inner nectar touches the tongue, the taste buds become extremely refined; then, even if you eat the simplest food, you relish it as pure elixir. When the inner nectar travels down to the gastric fire in the solar plexus, it spreads through all the nerves. This nectar nourishes the body so that it is not necessary to consume much food.

In this way the Kundalini purifies each of the five sense organs and invests them with divine powers. In order to develop these supersensory powers, the yogic scriptures prescribe specific techniques of concentration on the respective sensory nerves. But through the processes of Siddha Yoga, the Kundalini, of Her own accord, purifies each sense organ in a natural way. The Shakti gives one control over the senses. Then one is unaffected by the pull of outer sense objects, being firmly established in one's own nature, completely fulfilled within oneself. At this stage one has the experience of *pratīka-darshan*, the vision of one's own form. This phenomenon has great significance. It indicates that the body has been completely purified.

The Attainment

In the center of the sahasrara, there is a triangle, which one sees in meditation, and in the center of this triangle resides supreme Shiva, who is also called the supreme Guru. This is the goal of the Kundalini's journey. When the Kundalini reaches the sahasrara, She plays, and as She does so, She makes the knowledge arise in you that everything is the play of God. This is called pure knowledge, or *shuddha vidyā*, in Shaivism; the *Shiva Sūtras* say that when this pure knowledge arises in you, you attain Godhood.

As the Kundalini rises to the sahasrara, you begin to see a divine effulgence. There are one thousand knots in the sahasrara, which shine with the brilliance of a thousand suns, but instead of being scorching like the sun, their light is cooling. This light is so powerful that when it reveals itself to you, you don't have the strength to stand it. When I saw that brilliance within myself, I fell down, because I could not bear its intensity. In the center of that effulgence lies a tiny and fascinatingly beautiful light, the Blue Pearl, and when your meditation deepens you begin to see it, sparkling and scintillating. Sometimes it comes out of the eyes and stands in front of you. It moves with the speed of lightning, and it is so subtle that when it passes through the eye, the eye doesn't feel its movement.

Blue Pearl

41

The vision of the Blue Pearl is the most significant of all the experiences I have described. Everyone should see this Blue Pearl at least once. The scriptures describe this Blue Pearl as the divine light of Consciousness, which dwells within everyone. It is the actual form of the Self, our innermost reality, the form of God which lives within us. The Blue Pearl is subtler than the subtlest. It is the size of a sesame seed. Yet even though it is so tiny, it is very big, for this whole world of movable and immovable things is contained within it. The seed of a banyan tree is so small that if you take it in your fingers and crush it, it is gone. However if you sow that seed, then a big banyan tree springs forth from it, and in the banyan tree are infinite other seeds. In the same way, within the Blue Pearl are millions and millions of universes. The Blue Pearl contains the entire cosmos.

Having perceived this truth directly, Tukaram Maharaj, a great saint of India, wrote, "The Lord of the universe builds a tiny house the size of a sesame seed and lives inside it. All the different Gods — Brahma, Vishnu, and Mahesh — come up and go inside this tiny house."

Why should you meditate? Why should you awaken your inner Shakti? The answer is, to see this Blue Pearl. This is the goal of your spiritual journey. It is the Blue Pearl which puts an end to your bondage and makes you realize your own perfection.

You should practice meditation systematically and regularly. You may not have a high experience the first year, the second year, or the third year, but if you keep on meditating you will certainly experience the blue light one day. Don't be in a hurry. After all, you work for years to get degrees such as a B.A., M.A., PH.D., or M.D. After the Shakti has performed all its various functions and purified you thoroughly, you will be able to see the Blue Pearl. It will appear before you in meditation. But your meditation is not completed just by seeing the Blue Pearl. It has to become steady. If you have intense longing for God, deep love for your Guru, deep faith in Kundalini, there will come a time when you will be able to make the Blue Pearl stand still in front of you. Within it, you will see the deity you love. If you love Ram, you will see Ram. If you love Krishna, you will see Krishna. If you love Jesus, you will see Jesus. In our tradition, a lot of emphasis is placed on the personal form of God, and this experience is known as the realization of God with form. *saguna brahman*

One day, as my meditation was approaching its culmination, the Blue Pearl began to expand, until it was the size of a human being. The form of this Being was not made of flesh but of shimmering blue light, the blue light of Consciousness. He was exquisitely beautiful. He stood before me, a shimmering mass of Consciousness, and as I watched Him, I was wonderstruck. He made a sign to me with His eyes, and then began to speak.

"I see everything from everywhere," He said. "I see with my eyes, I see with my nose, I have eyes everywhere." He lifted His foot, and said, "I see with this foot. I have tongues everywhere. I can speak not just with my tongue but with every part of my body. I can move wherever I like. I can go anywhere in an instant. I walk without feet and catch without hands. I speak without a tongue, and I see without eyes. While I am far, far away, I am very near. I become the body in all bodies, and yet I am different from the body."

The Blue Person gave me some advice, and He gave me His blessing. Then, He reduced His form again to the Blue Pearl and entered within me.

I realized that this was the supreme unmanifest Being who is described in Chapter XI of the *Bhagavad Gītā*: "He has hands and feet everywhere. He has eyes, heads, and faces on all sides. He exists pervading all." It is this Being who grants the realization of God with form. This same Blue Being gives the command to become a Guru. Only one who has been commanded by his own Guru and by this Being can become a Guru.

The vision of the Blue Being is not the end of your journey. Finally, as you meditate and meditate, one day the Blue Pearl will explode, and its light will fill the universe, and you will experience your all-pervasiveness. This experience is the culmination of sadhana, the ultimate realization. In this state, you lose the awareness of your own body and merge with the body of God. It was when he became absorbed in the intoxication of this state of divinity that the great Sufi saint Mansur Mastana said, *ana'l-Haqq,* "I am God." It was after experiencing this that the great Shankaracharya proclaimed with firm conviction, "I am Shiva."

The truth is, this very body is the temple of God. There is no greater temple than this human body. Everyone should contemplate this and understand that God lies within him. Just as one says, "This is my property," or "This is my house," one should earn the right to say, "God is within me." Tukaram Maharaj said, "I went to look for God, but didn't find God. I myself became God. In this very body, God revealed Himself to me." And this is absolutely true.

This is the knowledge that arises as Kundalini merges in the sahasrara. This is the state of Parabhakti, supreme devotion, in which there is no devotee, no God, and no world, but only oneness. Just as a river, after flowing for a long time, merges in the ocean and becomes the ocean, when Kundalini has finished Her work and stabilized in the sahasrara, you become completely immersed in God. All your impurities and coverings are destroyed, and you take complete rest in the Self. The veil which made you see duality drops away, and you experience the world as a blissful play of Kundalini, a sport of God's energy. You see the universe as supremely blissful light, undifferentiated from yourself, and you remain unshakable in this awareness. This is the state of liberation, the state of perfection.

A being who has attained this state does not have to close his eyes and retire to a solitary place to get into samadhi. Whether he is meditating, eating, bathing, sleeping, whether he is alone or with others, he experiences the peace and joy of the Self. Whatever he sees is God, whatever he hears is God, whatever he tastes is God, whatever words he speaks are God's. In the midst of the world, he experiences the solitude of a cave, and in the midst of people, he experiences the bliss of samadhi. This is the state which the *Shiva Sūtras* describe as *lokānandah samādhisukham*, "The bliss of the world is the ecstasy of samadhi."[9]

It is to attain this that we should meditate, that we should have our Kundalini awakened. We do not meditate to attain God, because we have already attained Him. We meditate so that we can become aware of God manifest within us. This is the knowledge of Siddha Yoga, the fruit of the inner yoga which is activated when Kundalini is awakened by the grace of a perfect Master.

And this is why I always tell everyone, "Meditate on your Self, honor your Self, worship your Self, for God dwells within you as you."

NOTES

1. Elaine Pagels, *The Gnostic Gospels* (New York: Random House, 1979).

2. Frank Waters, *Book of the Hopi* (New York: Penguin Books, 1977), 11-12.

3. Ibid., 33.

4. *Shiva Sūtras* 1:13.

5. Kshemaraj, *Shiva Sūtra Vimarshini*.

6. *Shiva Sūtras* 1:18.

7. *Pratyabhijñāhridayam* 17.

8. Kallata, *Tattvartha Chintāmani*.

9. *Shiva Sūtras* 1:18.

GLOSSARY

ājñā **chakra**
the spiritual center located between the eyebrows described as a two-petaled lotus. The awakened Kundalini passes through this chakra only at the command (ajna) of the Guru. It is also referred to as the Guru chakra since the inner Guru can be envisioned here in the form of a shining flame.

bandha
(lit., "lock") a type of exercise in hatha yoga which, when practiced along with *prānāyāma* (breathing exercises), aids in uniting the *prāna* and *apāna* (outgoing and incoming breath). Bandhas also help to seal the prana in the body during the practice of *mudrās*. These techniques may also occur very naturally by the inspiration of the awakened Kundalini.

Bhagavad Gītā
one of the essential scriptures of Indian philosophy; the spiritual teachings of Lord Krishna in which he instructs his disciple Arjuna on the nature of God, the universe, and the Self, on the different forms of yoga, and on the way to attain God.

bhakti **yoga**
a path to Self-realization in which the primary focus is the expression of devotion to God; hence, it is known as the yoga of divine love.

bodily humors
wind, bile, and phlegm. According to the ancient Indian science of medicine, good health depends upon maintaining an even balance of these three substances.

Brahma
in Vedantic philosophy, this deity is the embodiment of the principle of creation.

chakra
(lit., "wheel") a center of conscious energy located in the subtle

47

body where the *nādīs* converge in such a way as to give the appearance of a lotus. There are six main chakras located in the *sushumnā* (central) nadi. Kundalini lies coiled at the base of the sushumna in the *mūlādhāra* chakra. When awakened, Kundalini begins to ascend through the sushumna, piercing all the chakras until She merges in the *sahasrāra*, the topmost spiritual center.

Chit
(Chiti) (1) divine conscious energy; (2) the active or creative aspect of God; the power which manifests the universe.

hatha yoga
this yoga derives its name from the Sanskrit *ha* (sun) and *tha* (moon); it involves the attainment of the *samādhi* state through the systematic balancing of the solar and lunar *prānas* which flow respectively through the *pingalā* and *idā nādīs* of the human body. By the diligent performance, under expert supervision, of physical exercises which include *āsanas* (postures), *mudrās* (seals), *bandhas* (locks), *kriyās* (cleansing practices), and *prānāyāma* (breath control), the adept hatha *yogi* carefully manages to merge the pranas flowing through ida and pingala and cause them to flow into the central nadi (*sushumnā*) instead. When this energy rises to the *sahasrāra*, it brings the experience of Self-realization.

idā
the *nādī* or subtle channel which extends from the *mūlādhāra* to the *ājñā chakra* running alongside the *sushumnā* and terminating above the base of the left nostril. The ida is referred to as the moon nadi because of its cooling nature.

japa
the repetition of a mantra, usually in silence.

jñāna yoga
the path of knowledge; the yoga of attaining supreme wisdom through intellectual inquiry.

karma yoga
the yoga of performing selfless action as service to God.

Kashmir Shaivism
nondualistic philosophy that recognizes the entire universe as a manifestation of Chiti, or divine conscious energy. Kashmir Shaivism explains how the unmanifest supreme Principle manifests as the universe.

khechari mudrā
a very advanced yogic mudra in which the tip of the tongue curls back into the throat and upward into the nasal pharynx. This mudra breaks the *rudragranthi* (knot of Rudra) in the *sushumnā nādī*, permitting the Kundalini to rise to the *sahasrāra*, causing the meditator to experience *samādhi*

states and taste divine nectar. In hatha yoga this mudra requires many years of arduous preparation, but in Siddha Yoga it occurs spontaneously at the command of the inner Guru.

Krishna
(lit., "the dark one") an incarnation of God who took birth to relieve the world of sin and unrighteousness. His life story is described in the Indian scriptures. See: Bhagavad Gītā.

kriyā
a gross (physical) or subtle (mental, emotional) purificatory movement initiated by the awakened Kundalini. Kriyas purify the body and nervous system so as to allow a seeker to endure the energy of higher states of consciousness.

kumbhaka
in hatha yoga, this refers to the holding of the breath after inhalation during the practice of *prāṇāyāma*. Esoterically, true kumbhaka occurs when the inward and outward flow of prana becomes stabilized. When this happens, the mind also stabilizes, permitting the meditator to experience the Self which lies beyond.

laya yoga
the yoga of attaining *samādhi* through meditative practices leading to the absorption of the

mind into the Self by listening to the divine inner sounds.

lock
See: bandha.

Mahesh
a name for Shiva, meaning great lord. See also: Shiva.

mantra
(1) sacred word or cosmic sound invested with the power of God; (2) God in the form of sound.

mudrā
(lit., "seal") (1) a hatha yoga technique practiced to hold the *prāna* within the body, forcing the Kundalini to flow into the *sushumnā* (central *nādī*). Mudras can occur spontaneously after receiving Shaktipat; (2) a symbolic gesture of movement of the hands which expresses inner feelings and inner states, or which conveys various qualities such as charity, knowledge, and fearlessness.

mūlādhāra chakra
the chakra at the base of the spine where Kundalini lies coiled. From here, Kundalini controls all the activities of the physiological system through its network of 720 million channels (*nādīs*). See also: chakra.

nāda
divine music or sounds which are heard in higher states of meditation.

nādī

a channel through which life-force is circulated through the human body. In the physical body, nadis take the form of blood vessels, nerves, and lymph ducts; in the subtle body they constitute a complex system of 720 million astral tubes through which the *prāna* flows. Of these, the most important nadis are *idā*, *pingalā* and *sushumnā*, described under separate listings.

pingalā

the *nādī* or subtle channel which extends from the *mūlādhāra* to the *ājñā chakra* running alongside the *sushumnā* and terminating above the base of the right nostril. The pingala is referred to as the sun nadi because of its heating nature.

prāna

(1) life-breath, the vital force of the body and universe which sustains life and is the power of animation; (2) the outgoing breath; (3) in the human body, yoga divides *prāna* into five types according to the functions it performs: prana controls the breath, *apāna* controls the elimination of waste matter, *samāna* distributes nourishment, *vyāna* moves the body parts, and *udāna* is the upward force in the *sushumnā* and is the power which, when activated, impels us upward toward Self-realization.

prānāyāma

the yogic science through which the *prāna* or vital force is brought under control and stabilized, a necessary condition in the instigation of the Self-realization process. In hatha yoga, pranayama is achieved through specific breathing exercises, since there is a link between the physical breath and the subtle prana. In Siddha Yoga, pranayama occurs spontaneously through the inner workings of the awakened Kundalini and is often attended by automatic changes in the breathing pattern during Siddha Yoga Meditation.

Pratyabhijñāhridayam

(lit., "the heart of the doctrine of recognition")
a concise treatise of twenty aphorisms which summarizes the philosophy of Kashmir Shaivism. In essence it states that due to wrong identification man has forgotten his true nature. It explains the nature of Absolute Reality, and teaches that Realization is a process of recognizing that truth. *See also:* Kashmir Shaivism.

rāja yoga

(1) the yoga of eight steps, or limbs, directed toward the purification and control of the mind, through which the Self is realized; (2) the supreme state attained by practicing raja yoga.

sādhanā
the practice of spiritual
discipline.

sahasrāra
the topmost spiritual center
described as a thousand-petaled
lotus located in the crown of the
head. It is the seat of Shiva, the
supreme Guru. As Kundalini
travels up the *sushumnā* and
merges with the sahasrara, the
individual soul attains the state
of *samādhi*.

samādhi
a transcendental state of awareness in which one experiences
the Supreme Reality and
becomes Self-realized. This state
occurs when the topmost *chakra*,
sahasrāra, is activated. There are
different types of samadhi
depending upon the degree of
activation and the type of yoga
employed. In Siddha Yoga, the
samadhi state is not attended by
unconsciousness to the external
world; rather, one experiences
sahaja (natural) samadhi, in
which one remains fully alert
and perceives the all-pervasiveness of universal Consciousness
throughout all daily activities.

sarvāngāsana
(whole-body pose) A hatha yoga
posture which is performed by
inverting the body until its
weight rests squarely on the
shoulders.

Shaivism
See: Kashmir Shaivism.

Shaktipat *dīkshā*
a yogic initiation in which the
Siddha Guru transmits his spiritual energy into the aspirant,
thereby awakening the aspirant's
dormant Kundalini. There are
four different ways in which
Shaktipat can be received: *sparsha*
diksha, through the Guru's physical touch; mantra diksha,
through his words; *drik* diksha,
through his look; and *manasa*
diksha, through his thoughts.

shambhavi *dīkshā*
the rarest of spiritual initiations
in which, as the result of receiving Shaktipat from a Siddha
Guru, an aspirant immediately
experiences the Supreme Reality.

Shankaracharya *(788-820)*
the great Indian philosopher
and saint known as a *jagadguru*
(world-Guru). He expounded
the philosophy of absolute non-
dualism, known as Advaita
Vedanta.

shīrshāsana
(headstand pose) a hatha yoga
posture performed with the body
completely inverted, the weight
centered squarely on the crown
of the head, and the spine prop-
erly aligned. When practiced
with expert guidance, this pose
becomes a *mudrā* which is very
effective in directing *prāna* into

the *sushumnā nāḍī*. In Siddha Yoga this pose may occur spontaneously with the awakening of Kundalini.

Shiva
a name for the all-pervasive Supreme Reality, the conscious inner Self. In his personal form he is revered as the lord of *yogis* and is known as the supreme Guru from whom the lineage of Gurus descends. He revealed and expounded various scriptures known as Agamas, among them the scriptures of Kashmir Shaivism and the tantras.

Shiva Sūtras
a Sanskrit text consisting of seventy-seven aphorisms which were inscribed by Lord Shiva on a rock in Kashmir and revealed to the sage Vasuguptacharya in the ninth century. Beginning with the aphorism "The Self is Consciousness," it is the scriptural authority and basis for the philosophical school of Kashmir Shaivism.

Siddha
perfected one, one who has attained the state of unity-awareness, who experiences himself as all-pervasive, and who has achieved mastery over his senses and their objects.

sushumnā
the primary *nāḍī* of the subtle body, running up the center of the spinal axis. It is the only nadi which connects all six *chakras* with the *sahasrāra*, the abode of Shiva at the crown of the head, and thus it is through this nadi that the Shakti must flow before Self-realization can be attained. Within sushumna is an even smaller nadi known as *chitriṇī*, and this is the actual conduit through which the Kundalini rises. Sushumna is also called the *brahma* nadi (channel of the Absolute), the *samvitti* nadi (channel of Consciousness), and the Pathway of the Great Kundalini.

tandrā
a meditation state resembling a deep-sleep state but often accompanied by spiritual visions, precognition, astral travel, and other such supranormal experiences.

three knots
(*granthis*) the three junction points in the *sushumnā* (central *nāḍī*) where the *idā*, *pingalā*, and sushumna nadi converge and form a knot. They are: *brahmagranthi* — located in the *mūlādhāra chakra*; *vishnugranthi* — located in the heart chakra; and *rudragranthi* — located in the *ājñā* chakra. The awakened Kundalini pierces through these knots as She ascends sushumna to the *sahasrāra*.

Tukaram Maharaj *(1608-1650)*
a great poet-saint of Maharashtra,
India, who received spiritual initiation in a dream. He composed
thousands of devotional songs
describing all aspects of spiritual
life, which are revered as scriptural authority.

Upanishads
the knowledge of the ancient
sages, based on their direct experience of supreme Truth, which
teaches that the Self of man is
the same as the Absolute.

Vishnu
a name for one aspect of the all-
pervasive Supreme Reality; this
personal form represents God as
the sustaining principle of the
universe.

yoga
(lit., "union") (1) the state of
oneness with the Self, God;
(2) the practices and spiritual
disciplines leading to that state.

yogi; yogin
(1) one who practices yoga;
(2) one who has attained the
goal of yogic practices.

Further Reading

by Swami Muktananda

Play of Consciousness
From the Finite to the Infinite
Where Are You Going?
I Have Become Alive
The Perfect Relationship
Reflections of the Self
Secret of the Siddhas
I Am That
Mystery of the Mind
Does Death Really Exist?
Light on the Path
In the Company of a Siddha
Lalleshwari
Siddha Meditation
Bhagawan Nityananda
Mukteshwari
Meditate

by Swami Chidvilasananda

My Lord Loves a Pure Heart
Kindle My Heart
Ashes at My Guru's Feet

You may learn more about the teachings and
practices of Siddha Yoga Meditation by contacting:

SYDA Foundation
371 Brickman Road, PO Box 600,
South Fallsburg, NY 12779-0600, USA
(914) 434-2000

or

Gurudev Siddha Peeth
P.O. Ganeshpuri
PIN 401 206
District Thana
Maharashtra, India

For further information about books in print
by Swami Muktananda and Swami Chidvilasananda,
and editions in translation, please contact:

Siddha Yoga Meditation Bookstore
371 Brickman Road, PO Box 600,
South Fallsburg, NY 12779-0600, USA
Tel: (914) 434-0124